Kitty Coles

Seal Wife

Indigo Dreams Publishing

First Edition: Seal Wife
First published in Great Britain in 2017 by:
Indigo Dreams Publishing Ltd
24 Forest Houses
Halwill
Beaworthy
EX21 5UU
www.indigodreams.co.uk

ISBN 978-1-910834-57-2

British Library Cataloguing in Publication Data. A CIP record
for this book can be obtained from the British Library.

Designed and typeset in Palatino Linotype by Indigo Dreams.
Cover design by Ronnie Goodyer at Indigo Dreams

Printed and bound in Great Britain by: 4edge Ltd.
www.4edge.co.uk

Papers used by Indigo Dreams are recyclable products made
from wood grown in sustainable forests following the guidance
of the Forest Stewardship Council.

for Douggie, for ever and ever

Thanks are due to the editors of the following magazines where some of these poems have already appeared:

Amaryllis, Clear Poetry, Envoi, Ink Sweat and Tears, Iota, Monkey Kettle, Obsessed With Pipework, Sarasvati, South, The Cro Magnon, The Fat Damsel, The Fenland Reed, The Frogmore Papers, The Interpreter's House, The Journal, The Lake, The Seventh Quarry, Three Drops from a Cauldron.

This is Kitty's first collection.

CONTENTS

Forest

Either you don't go into the dark forest
or you go
and go unarmed.

Its depths are thick with vampires:
this is known.
Go in attended with the crucifix,
garlic, mirrors,
all tried remedies,
and you won't meet them.

You may glimpse them regarding you
palely from a distance.
There was no point in leaving home for that.

Walk in unarmed.
You'll pass the witch's cottage.
The wolves, the ghouls,
will track you. Close your eyes
and feel the darkness rush
with all its wings.
Submit
to it
and feel it lift you, take you,
and feel its teeth meet there,
beneath the skin.

Now you're acquainted.
Now see the ghost
of yourself which will teach you
how to live here unafraid.

The Doe-Girl

She had always been timid,
reticent, secretive,
wide-eyed, easily startled
by sudden noises,
thin-legged, fond of woodland,
prone to running.

One day, she sensed a pressure
in the skull. Antlers
emerged, puny at first,
malformed.
Her ears lengthened
and her eyes, once blue,
turned black all over,
like ink spreading through water.

Now, we glimpse her sometimes,
moving between tree-trunks,
across clearings,
wary, at a distance.
Her hooves leave tracks,
like tidy hearts, behind.
She vanishes, silent,
among leaves,
dapples of light.
We don't think she knows us
any more.

The Seeds Of The Pomegranate

have a perfumed flavour, biting and luscious,
streak the wrists with fluid.
Their juice marks cloth almost indelibly.

We share a fruit. You halve it and the blade
forces apart the grisly mass of jewels.
You hack, they bleed, fight to retain their wholeness.

You feed me arils from your guilty fingers.
Their smell is winey, green, but I think
of my flesh, the cysts beading its centre.

My mother scours the city
as we lie here. I am lost to her light.
My mouth is full of your gift.

A Soul

Is that your soul you hold in your hand,
as small as a walnut
and equally weazen?
Who knows how many years it's seen,
owl pellet, pitted bullet,
black ball, bounced back?
Who knows how many attempts
it's survived, what tower-scalers,
what goblin-slayers, what occult assailants?

Yes, you say, it is. Just that.
You are looking for somewhere
to leave it.
The old box is too dry,
too arid a zone, riddled now with toxicity.
You are hoping for a new home.

You would have me open my mouth
and swallow it,
dark bolus, bad bean.
It would lodge in my stomach,
lodge in and nestle,
a dainty mouse seeking shelter.

From you, I have learned sleight of hand.
I stash it under my tongue,
unwanted, almighty pill.
Later, I will let it roll into the corner
for dust to settle on,
or the cat to play with,
or the legs of the chairs to obliterate.

If it meant a thing to me now
I would squash it myself.

Luminous

You've circled my dreams all night,
a swarm of yourself,
o pearly one, hatched clean
from your bed of grit.

I have stumbled upon
your white body saved from the sea.
The sand where you twitched,
lying mute, impeded my way.

Cool maggot, you insinuate yourself
into the fabric of the house,
its breathing, exhaling your marshland
vapours through the ceilings.

This trickle I hear is the steady,
the stealthy, water tracing dark lines
down the walls. I lean to lick it.
You do not taste as fresh as you once did.

You have been dead. Godlike,
you live again. Your second coming
is ruinous to my order. Your grave clothes,
on the floor, shine, luminous.

Exorcism

All day, you scurry about with your little net,
like a hunter of moths, things of darkness,
duplicitous fire. You are diligent
in your efforts. You search them down
and slaughter them on the spot, steadfast and efficient.

The house hums with your work. Their black blood
is scentless. You scrub it from the floors.
The wood wears thin. I rest on the sofa.
You bring me lemon water. You wrap me in blankets.
I am only warm when you hold me.

All night, the wind slathers the house
in wet, throws leaves like the plumage
of tropical birds at the windows.
You sleep, so I become the one who hunts.
I keep myself awake by speaking your name.

Waking, you say I'm pale, my eyes
are bruised by my vigils.
I am earning my place here. Some day
I will deserve you. My body quivers,
waiting for your flame.

The Butcher's Wife

His hands are white as a princess's,
or milk, so the network of veins
shows through as clear as a blueprint.

They are cold, like the petals of lilies,
marble-cool. The nails are kept short.
He uses a brutal brush

to scour under them. Then he files
them smooth as shells. They are pink
like sweeties, like fondant, like blushing brides.

In the evenings, I sit on the sofa, try not to watch
those hands constructing exquisite butterflies
from origami paper, one after another.

Their movements are as intricate
as ballet, caress the paper, gentle as a lover,
each fold precise, in its own way, as surgery.

At night, those hands are on me.
They smell like blood, a rusty vehemence
infecting the heat of the bedroom.

I dream of skeins of bunnies, the sides
of cows, the skin peeled off,
those hands parting my ribs.

Green Girl

If I hold still enough,
stare long enough
at the candle flame's
black smokes like veils,
can I arrest
the scutter of
my rabbit heart,
the flow of my bad blood,
suspend my breath?

Looking until
I meld myself
with light, can I
wait out this time
of rain and darkness,
arriving at the spring
no longer sick?

Can I retreat
from winter, shrinking,
shrinking – only
my hair and nails
still lengthening –
lapse from myself
till the return
of warmer days
waken with vine-leaves
coiling at my head,
casing my heart,
leaves rising from
my lungs, emerging
bit by bit from
open lips, tongue thick
with bursting buds?

Black Annis

It's a fine place I have here, this bower
of rag and bone. A squadron
of eyes studs the ceiling,
reflects, a jellied mirror, quiver
on marbly quiver,
blue skin and nails of iron.

An intricate décor, then,
with a quirky feel of its own
and a smell – rather,
perfume – that's hard to put a name to.
It's a shame there's little
to hear. It seems there are no birds around.

It's good to know what one is. I am known
as a horror. My gowns
of skin, beloved scarves,
repulse you. Since you told me so,
I have never been the same woman. You refuse
to believe that I could be a good mother

But my children stay with me,
in me, forever and ever.
You let your children
run wild. They are lost forever. I take them
home, protect them from foul weather,
dark nights, the wicked
things that walk in them.

The Growing Of A Witch

For a long time, I was not a remarkable person.
The change came slowly; I could hardly see it –

with my weak eyes – at first, though I
heard a beating of the air

with smothery things like wings.
Then it got in my throat. The feathers

brushed my tongue when I tried to speak.
They sieved my dinner. Veins rose

in my hands. The skin grew thin and milky.
Old scars tunnelled like maggots. I grew

an owl's bill. After that, I broke the mirrors.
The splinters were water, sploshing

light like paint up the walls, gemming the floor.
I took in an imp, feeding her like the pelican

must feed its brood, on blood.
It was not my intention

to cause alarm. My herbs, my hexes,
were never left on your doorstep.

I never wanted to hurt you. I thought you knew
that. Your chains, your irons, your fires say otherwise.

Poltergeist

Now I enter your house.
I breathe myself through your loose window seals
and under doors. I deliver myself,
with a thump, through the letterbox.

Un-vampirelike, I need no invitation,
though once you used to call
at any hour and wake me
with your urgency to hear me,

whisper endearments, beg me to come over.
I whisper now, and lean
upon your shoulder, and pinch
your flinching forearms.

You bruise so easily! I used to think your kisses
would scald and mark me,
the heat of them lasting
hours after you had left me.

On the steam of the bathroom mirror,
I write your name, and mine,
entwine them in a kind of monogram.
I lift your plates

and break them on the wall.
The day you went, I did nothing at all.
I didn't speak or sob. I watched you go.
You took the greater part of me with you.

Life Undead

You'll find it's the taste of blood that you never get used to,
 its slick trickle, the rust that lingers in the throat.
And the lack of give in their skin as your teeth

meet there it can make it hard to steel yourself to drink.
The thirst is constant, a curse, a low-grade
ache. You must stop yourself from gazing

too long at their necks. You'll surmise that your heart
has a little door that snaps shut. It is this
that allows you to close out the things they tell you

in the time you spend alone
when you've charmed them back
to the rented room, the hotel, the empty flat.

You will change your name.
migrate, fudge your CV, to hide how long
you survive, your non-decay.

In the absence of a grim ancestral pile
in the Carpathians, you find yourself
working all hours to pay the bills, the rent;

inheritances spent, pension unfeasible.
The limited blessings: you scarcely need to sleep,
you have the strength of ten, are never sick.

You will practice meditation to pass the time,
to set outside that door in your heart
the instinct to die.

The Huntsman's Wife

In the dark of the year, I find you waiting always
at the stable door, your black coat on, your hat
in your hand as you scuff the muddy straw.
Your old horse is accustomed to your habits.
He has woken himself and his breath damps both our faces.

Good wife, I brush and comb him like a child.
Sparks fly from him. My thick boots stamp them down.
I pick his hooves for grits and nubs of sky.
I fetch the saddle, cool beneath my hand.
I bridle him. You nod to me and mount.

Out in the yard, the air is stiff with stars.
You pull me down a handful. They melt like ice
between our palms and slither from my fingers.
I wait until the clouds have rolled between us.
I wait all night to see the soul you'll bring me.

Osiris

I find a slipper under the sofa.
I study the bed for stray hairs, comb the scurf
of skin from your desk, invisible
but potent nonetheless.
I am glad of the curlings of fingernail
left in the bathroom.
If I only knew where you
had misplaced your heart.
The little red thing has hopped off
with a mind of its own.

I grow you again, through words,
through silence,
through watching. Your skin
sprouts green. Your hair is a field of wheat.
You are cold to the touch, like a fish.
like a fish, damp and gooey.
When your tongue was lost the cat
must've got at the edges.
You speak haltingly.
Dense lichen covers your fingers.

I am your witch, your wife, your supplicant.
Looking back, I was foolish to think you'd be the same.

Lighthouse Keeper

At night, the light is orange on the water,
and the water black.
I watch the seals emerging by the rocks,
owl eyed, round-headed as children.
The sheen of their flanks
is oily, voluptuous. I watch
all night but you are never among them.

By day, I trim the wicks,
burnish the lens, the windows' fire.
I wind the clocks. I mount the attic stairs
and lift your pelt from the chest
and finger its satin, inhale
its briny odour, the scent of tears.
You have taken your pelt.
There is nothing under my fingers.
I know you will never
return to me by sunlight.

All night, the seabirds cry,
'Come back, come back.'
Their words reverberate in the rift
you have opened
beneath my ribs, into which
my days are slipping.
The sea strikes the rocks,
echoes, 'Come back, come back.'

Seal Wife

The weather turns.
A wind from the north has flown in,
with its violent curse,
and it raises the waves
till I cannot shut out their yowling.

The old scars itch on my flank,
disquieted.
The hairs on my spine rise up
in the chill that presses
itself under the door,
an insinuating ghost.

The cat has wound herself
to an endless running
from one end of the house to the other,
poor bristling devil.

The grass is aching with frost.
Birds fall, small toys,
from the trees in their deaths.
The cold is murderous.

In the churchyard, the drowned
walk at noon as if it were night.
They return to old beds,
slip in by their frozen wives.

And I am numbing myself
with my baking, my stitching, by washing
the floors till the stone begins to thin.
I hide my face from the mirror:
its enquiry threatens.
If I could forget, the water could not claim me.

Bluebeard

Words are blunt implements that can't convey
precise degrees of longing, acquiescence,
consent bound up inside a No, a Yes.
Words are like nuts the peckish must crack open.
The tender, hidden part's the part worth having.

I have made a lifelong study of the meanings
obscured within a nod, a look, a shake.
I have mastered the art of talking by touch only,
bypassing speech to hear the response in her wrist.
Like crystal balls, her eyes uncloud, inform me.
Her blue dress tells me more than her red dress.

I'm familiar now with the secrets unloosed
by the body, wishes adherent in each part of it.
I differentiate from other paleness
the paleness that wants to be darkened,
from other softness
the softness that asks to be crushed.

Third Wife

He displays this one's bones in a case, like a dinosaur's.
They are yellow and strong and clean
and chipped and pitted.

Her head is shiny and silent, a head of wax.
It floats like a candle flame,
serene, impassive.

The second one's heart
is kept in a jar on a sill,
preserved in aspic for posterity.

Her tongue, he stores in a reliquary,
with a twist of old hair
as yellow as my own.

And I, I feel no fear,
I do not flinch, when he guides me in
to look and pinches my flesh,

leaving bruises the colour of doves,
the size of petals.
These artefacts of the past do not deter me.

He never misses kissing me goodnight.
He tells me only I know how to please him.
He loves me like he never loved the others.

Widow

Past those nightly dreams of seeking
you, running immeasurable space, calling your name
and waking with the echo of the cry.

Now dreaming you back into existence, forming
your face, your limbs, like buds,
inside me. Now with you the whole night through.

Still waking shocked to find your absence
living in our house, lying
in wait, crying itself far louder than a presence.

Still lying still, clenching my eyes against
the sight, the scent, of nothing on your side,
my ears against the silence of your breath.

Stepmother

The mirror shows the creases
by my eyes, circling my neck, are spreading,
unmistakably spreading. Its speechless pool
is imperturbable, reflects the truth,
delineates the facts.

I touch my belly's curve: it does not dimple.
This water will not part,
will not enfold me.
Unwholesome with love,
I turn heretical. I will construct
a new veracity.

Last night, someone told me that my blood
was perfume.
I'll turn the mirrors' faces to the wall.
I'll live on swallows to restore my youth.

Peter, The Wild Boy

I have no words but words are not everything.
There are stones. There is water.
These must mean something.
Even in a house
there are stones and water.

Darkness is a happening: it signifies something.
They can stop darkness. They make heat appear.
I think this must mean they have stolen the meanings.

I had nothing at all but I sense
they have taken something.
In walls it is harder to hear the cry of the morning.
It is harder to smell the light, the flat sun rising.
It is harder to taste the blood of hot trees rising.

There are secret things here,
the small things still scurrying,
grey mice eating, mating, racing, dying.
Nobody sees the little mice like I can.

I am not mice,
of course. I am not like anything.
The men here are all ignorant
men like children.
They have never heard the pulse that runs
under everything.
They have never heard their own blood
ticking, ticking.

I am blood and bones in a sack.
I can hold this something.
I can taste the blood when I bite.
It is everything, everything.

Lir's Children

The lake's dark. Its mists
have fingers. Last year, it drowned a girl.
The water cleans her bones, lapping like cats.

We float and are cold.
Our feet catch like oars in the weed.
Time passes slowly when you have no words.

It is hard to accustom oneself
to a diet of tubers, of submerged plants,
to the weight and prickle of feathers.

We are white and still.
When we dive, it is gloomy and bony.
When we fly,

we ascend from a kingdom's cares,
a father's mourning.
Our wings batter the sky. We shake off the water
like stars.

Morrigan

The white death ray of the moon has nothing on you,
your blood-black, berry-black eyes, your lunar curves.
You are serpentine in velvet, in silk, in wool.
Your sleek lips sip at their wrists and throats like sickness.

The soft sweet voice of the sea has nothing on you,
your siren song, your smile, the depth of your treasure.
Your wrecks are dark and secret and full of pearls.
Your walk is a whisper, a licking of soles on satin.

The knife's slick bite through skin has nothing on you,
your smooth neat nick through flesh and cloth and bone.
You are home like a vault is home to hope and horror.
Your pets glide at your side, black feathers sighing.

Ceridwen

Skin pricking sore with sprouting of sleek fur,
the flesh recedes; the ribs uncase themselves.
I unleash, arrow-like, a hound in pursuit of a hare.

The limbs contract. The eyes ascend the skull.
Webs knit the fingers, tail thickening rudder-like.
I part the river, an otter hunting a fish.

Mouth hardening, lengthening, hooking itself,
while arms lighten and feather, lift me on dull air.
I hurl myself, a hawk chasing a dove.

Growths flapping from the chin, atop the head,
the torso plumps, the bill shrinks down again.
I scratch and cluck, a hen picking one grain.

The belly swells and slops with freight inside.
Heartsick, veins flaunting inky through breasts' white,
I plan a death, a woman vast with child.

Sack stitched tight shut, face like a flower inside,
the sound of screaming louder than the surf,
I launch my son, ship-like, upon the tide.

On The Capturing Of Ghosts

Like wasps, you lure them with something appetising,
the brine of tears, the metallic
tang of blood. Bait the jar and wait

for the liminal times – the dusk,
the dawn – when the veil is stretched to its thinnest
and death and life are porous,

their boundaries seeping.
Ghosts will congregate at crossroads, sweep
over the valleys, as visible

as mist, with their damp, their chilling.
Select the one you want. You will know
him by instinct, the feel of his breath

on your neck, his remembered odour.
(And of course you must choose
the bait of your jar to please him).

Then call him by name, the syllables
that still shape him, and invite him to taste:
ghosts are grateful for invitations.

He will make himself small, curling round
on himself like a hedgehog, and slip into
the jar and lick at the nourishment in there.

His attention held, take the lid and screw it tight.
Then bury the jar in earth, as if it were bone, and forget
his name. Let the weight slip from your shoulders.

Snow White

I have feared the body, its unmanageable reds,
persistent gripes of its bones,
its importunate
petitions for sustenance.
I've spent my days in striving
to contain it,
to make it conceal the evidence
of mortality, excrescences,
unseemly blemishes.

Now it's stopped dead. I lie in it like a bulb
in winter earth
tenaciously waiting for spring.
It has locked down its needs
to feed, excrete and bleed.
It is pale and cool and sweatless,
marmoreal doll.

I thought I would love to be odourless
as the angels, ascend
from preoccupations of the flesh.
But I learn to long
for another
kind of death. The wish
for my heart to hurt, to beat,
consumes me.

Homunculus

You were the best of all my progeny,
chip of my soul, a sprite of fire and air.
I watched you grow, I taught you how to be,
believed you pure as the breath I made you with,
blood of my blood, eyes wet with my own tears,
gave you my hair and nails, dear voodoo imp.

It was from love for you I turned you loose.
You bayed for freedom and I set you free
to scuttle like a leaf down night-time streets.
I feared the wind would blow you in the river,
feet stomp you flat, a starved cat gulp you down,
but set my fears aside to please you, heart-mouse.

Now you're full grown, o how you disappoint me!
You're dirty faced and pick up dirty habits.
Your words are scraped from gutters, dregs of bottles.
You strut like a cock on a muckheap, crow and cackle.
You're red of wattle, feet scabby as a pigeon's,
rat-toothed and greedy, muncher of old peelings.

Your clothes are heavy with ribbons, tawdry sequins,
you seize in your magpie fists and scarper with.
Your nails grow long and click like a dog's
as you beetle up walls, through windows,
in search of gewgaws. The sound of them scares
decent people indoors, closing their curtains.
O ram of many horns, o mucky baby,
o bull-bellied roarer, o my nasty pet!

Ragnarok

He will not go quietly, this old red autumn.
The sunsets burn like flares at the horizon.
The air is weighted with the stink of pyres.
Blight makes the leaves surrender, dry and fall.

The river has unseamed the banks and risen
across the fields, made moats around the trees.
Above the mountain, the clouds coagulate.
They turn themselves to blackness, choke the stars.

And we, revolving in our draughty heaven,
dwindle like wasps when winter thins their stores.
I will see you again on the other side of the water.
Our sustenance will be the morning dew.

Banshee

Shuffling dissatisfactions like my pack of cards,
I comb my hair. It is white,
fills the night like a vapour.

I arise
with a cry like an owl, like a child,
like a woman, who is not a woman, quite,

but the bones of your future.
In a silence that brims with shadow, that quivers
like water, I unreel myself

on the skein of my voice, my keening.
I am washing your bloody linen -
will it never be wholesome?

I am calling to warn you. I frighten
the birds from sleep but I fear
you do not listen.

A Journey

Already, the moon is full, the month of long nights.
Frost petrifies the grass; birds fall in sheaves.

Again, it's time to go down into the cave,
the echoey gut of the earth that slithers with shadow,

and there in its dark put on the shape of a bat
and hang so the blood flows down

to the head and feel the lift
of the air, though unmoving, suspended

in a cape of tarpaulin wings.
Wait long enough, till numbness covers the body,

till the pulse has slowed to the faintest
shiver of living. Then the eyes

will open and see what was unseen,
the shapes that breathe in the world-crypt,

their names and meanings.
Carry them home, wrapped tight in your arms

like gifts. Release their message;
let ice preserve its blessing.

Indigo Dreams Publishing
24 Forest Houses
Halwill
Beaworthy
Devon
EX21 5UU
www.indigodreams.co.uk